D1561020

CHRISTMAS

By
Madeline Tyler

BookLife PUBLISHING

©2021
BookLife Publishing Ltd.
King's Lynn
Norfolk, PE30 4LS

All rights reserved.
Printed in Malta.

A catalogue record for
this book is available from
the British Library.

ISBN: 978-1-83927-470-1

Written by:
Madeline Tyler

Edited by:
John Wood

Designed by:
Drue Rintoul

CONTENTS

Words that look like <u>this</u> can be found in the glossary on page 24.

CELEBRATE CHRISTMAS WITH ME!

My name is Eva and I am here to tell you all about Christmas.

Christmas is a time for families to come together and celebrate the birth of Jesus Christ. Come and celebrate with me!

CHRISTIANITY

Christmas is part of a religion called Christianity. Christianity began in the Middle East over 2,000 years ago. We believe that there is one God.

In some countries, presents are given on the 24th of December.

Christmas is a happy time. We see our friends and family and exchange presents. Presents are sometimes wrapped in colourful wrapping paper and decorated with ribbons.

THE STORY OF CHRISTMAS

Over 2,000 years ago in a place called Nazareth, a woman called Mary was visited by an angel. The angel told Mary that she would give birth to a baby called Jesus.

Mary was <u>engaged</u> to a man called Joseph. While she was <u>pregnant</u>, they travelled to Bethlehem to take part in a <u>census</u>. The journey was long and very difficult.

The Christmas story is sometimes called the Nativity.

When they got to Bethlehem, it was very busy with people returning for the census. The local <u>inn</u> was full, but the innkeeper said that they could stay in the stable where he kept his animals.

After Jesus was born, an angel helped some shepherds to find the stable. Three wise men from the East followed a star to Bethlehem. They gave Jesus gifts of gold, <u>frankincense</u> and <u>myrrh</u>.

We celebrate Christmas to remember Jesus, the Son of God.

ADVENT

Advent begins on the Sunday nearest to the 30th of November, and it is about <u>preparing</u> for Christmas Day.

Some children have advent calendars that help them count down to Christmas Day.

Some churches have an advent wreath. There are usually four candles, one for each Sunday leading up to Christmas Day. Some wreaths have a candle in the middle to light on Christmas Day.

CAROLS AND DECORATIONS

Some church services around Christmastime include carol singing. Christmas carols are happy songs that tell us about the Christmas story.

Presents are sometimes kept underneath a Christmas tree until Christmas Day.

Decorations are very popular around Christmas.
Towns and cities might put up decorations in the street, and some people put Christmas trees up in their homes.

CHRISTMAS EVE

The day before Christmas Day is called Christmas Eve. Some people may go to a church service called Christingle Service, where children light candles stuck into oranges. This is called a Christingle.

The candle in a Christingle represents Jesus's light in the world.

Another popular service held on Christmas Eve is Midnight Mass. There is praying and singing, and Christians celebrate Holy Communion.

Holy Communion is when Christians eat bread and drink wine to remember Jesus and what he did for the world.

CHRISTMAS DAY

Many people spend Christmas Day with their family. Some families go to church together on Christmas Day.

Friends and families exchange gifts and open any presents they have been given. Some people have stockings with presents inside that they open on Christmas Day.

Stocking

FESTIVE FOOD

Most families come together to eat a big meal on Christmas Day. A popular dish is roast turkey with vegetables.

In the UK, people usually eat Brussels sprouts, stuffing, roast potatoes and gravy.

Gingerbread houses are fun to make at Christmas. They can be decorated with icing and sweets.

CHRISTMAS AROUND THE WORLD

There are many Christians around the world and many ways of celebrating Christmas. The Giant Lantern Festival in San Fernando, Philippines, celebrates the start of the Christmas season.

I hope you have learnt a lot about Christmas! Why not see if there are any interesting Christmas celebrations in your area?

GLOSSARY

census	an official count of the people who live in a country or area
engaged	keeping a promise and plan to get married
frankincense	sticky stuff taken from a certain type of tree that is burnt to smell nice
inn	a house that can provide travellers with food, drink and a place to stay
myrrh	sticky stuff taken from a certain type of tree that is used as perfume or medicine
pregnant	when a woman has a baby growing inside her
preparing	getting ready
represents	stands for something else
service	religious act of praise to a god or gods, carried out in a particular order
worship	a religious act where a person shows their love for a god

INDEX